The Cliffs of New Alexandria, PA

Brian and Judi Lloyd

authorHOUSE

AuthorHouse™
1663 Liberty Drive
Bloomington, IN 47403
www.authorhouse.com
Phone: 1-800-839-8640

© 2012 Brian and Judi Lloyd. All rights reserved.

No part of this book may be reproduced, stored in a retrieval system, or transmitted by any means without the written permission of the author.

Published by AuthorHouse 5/21/2012

ISBN: 978-1-4685-6206-4 (sc)
ISBN: 978-1-4685-6205-7 (e)

Library of Congress Control Number: 2012904679

Any people depicted in stock imagery provided by Thinkstock are models, and such images are being used for illustrative purposes only. Certain stock imagery © Thinkstock.

This book is printed on acid-free paper.

Because of the dynamic nature of the Internet, any web addresses or links contained in this book may have changed since publication and may no longer be valid. The views expressed in this work are solely those of the author and do not necessarily reflect the views of the publisher, and the publisher hereby disclaims any responsibility for them.

Brian and Judi Lloyd

This book is dedicated to my brother:

DALE ALAN LLOYD
1955-2011

To Blackie Watt
Judi & Brown
June 17, 2012

A HISTORY IN STONE

We had seen the names etched in the cliffs along the Loyalhanna Creek, in New Alexandria, PA, years ago during one of our walks. We were fascinated by them because of the dates and years on some of them, and because we could associate them with people we knew in town.

We never really gave them another thought, other than mentioning about them to our neighbor, Jill, who told us stories about how her and the other kids in town would go down behind the town and climb around on the rocks, and that she remembered seeing the names, some of them being her ancestors.

This is a map of the borough of New Alexandria, PA.

In 2009, during another one of our walks along the trail at the base of the cliffs, we noticed that time and weather were having an adverse affect on the etchings, and on the cliffs themselves. Some of the names that had been carved in to the stone were worn to the point that they were impossible to make out, some were gone altogether; the rocks having flaked away or eroded away from the water flowing over them from above; and some of the overhanging rocks had fallen away from the main outcroppings.

A view of the trail along the base of the cliff.

We decided then that we were going to make several more trips back to locate and record as many of the etchings as possible before they were all gone forever.

We went back down in the Spring of 2010, and again in the Fall of 2011; the Fall of 2010 and the Spring of 2011 being too wet and rainy, which kept the Loyalhanna Creek over its banks, flooding the trail which provides the only access to the cliffside.

We photographed every etching we could find, most of them easily readable, and some that are impossible to read, but we photographed them in the hopes of deciphering them at a future time, but wanted to at least preserve what was left of them.

A photograph of "Signature Rock" along the Loyalhanna Creek

For some reason, the dates found on the Eastern end of the cliffs are the oldest, from the 1800's; and the ones at the Western end are the more recent, from the early 1900's. There is one large boulder, surrounded by several smaller ones, that sets along the water's edge, that has the majority of the etchings not found on the cliffs. We named this one "Signature Rock", which is in the photograph on the previous page.

A view of the cliffs where they start at the West end of town.

A photo of the cliffs about half way along the trail.

Most of the carvings are easily accessible, some take a little balancing and agility to reach because of soft ground and loose rock. The ones on Signature Rock can of course only be seen when the Loyalhanna Creek is within its banks, and then you will have to wash the mud and dirt off that has settled on them when the water was high.

All the etchings herein are found in the rocks from the West end of town to the East end behind Church Street, and are now part of the Army Corps of Engineers flood control ground for the Loyalhanna Dam, which is a few miles North of New Alexandria.

All the property along Church Street is privately owned, so the only access to the trail is through the flood control ground at the West end of town. The trail is on flat ground along the creek bank except in one section where the hill apparently slid down.

One photo showing the rocks that have broken from the cliff.

Access to the area is limited to dry days, and either in the early Spring, before any plants begin to grow, or in the Fall, after all the weeds die down and the leaves have fallen off the trees.

Another photo showing some of the large sections that have broken off the cliff.

Any other time is possible, but is sheer torture from the insects, mud, thick brush, and the relentless briars. Not to mention all the ashes from fireplaces and stoves that were emptied over the bank during the past two hundred years. They are several feet deep in places and provide very loose footing when trying to navigate along the cliffs.

Any attempts by anyone wishing to check this area out should be met with safety in mind. A good pair of high top shoes, gloves, and a long sleeve shirt would be advised. Care must be taken to avoid the many poison ivy vines that are growing everywhere.

A view of the cliffs about midway looking East, showing what is left of what used to be a very large overhang.

Some of the names are familiar to long time residents of New Alexandria; Sheffler, Fennell, Sligh, Felton, and King, are families that have been a part of its history since the 1800's. We did a little research on some of the names we found and have included some information on them throughout the book.

The area that would become New Alexandria was first settled in the mid 1700's, so when walking along the trail it is easy to imagine the early pioneers that came along here, hunting, fishing, and swimming; (the water was much cleaner then), and stopping to chisel their names and initials in the rocks to let future generations know that they had been here.

We have included various photographs of the Cliffside and also the terrain along the trail to give you an idea of what the area looks like. It is not a large area by any means, and what we refer to as "cliffs, would amount to a speed bump compared to the cliffs found in the Western United States.

Another view of the cliffs about midway looking West showing the largest surviving overhang.

At one time, there were some large overhanging rocks along the cliff. Large enough, as related to us by our neighbor Jill, that her and all her friends would gather under them and build a big fire. Not too much of the overhanging rock is present as seen in the accompanying photographs.

This photograph is of the cliff at its highest point, and also shows the many poison ivy vines that must be avoided.

The photograph above shows the cliffs towards the East end of town. The bank in the foreground, at the base of the cliff, was created by soil erosion from above, and also the flooding from the Loyalhanna Creek leaving layer after layer of soil each time it receded after flooding.

When the water is high it reaches right up to the base of the rock.

The photograph above shows the cliff at the West end of town where they begin. The trail starts here and is the easiest access to the cliffs.

The long narrow flat rock just off center in the photo contains most of the etchings found at this end, and can be seen in more detail in the photographs on the next few pages.

A closer view of the rock showing the etchings. A frame has been chiseled around them. Below is the upper left of the frame with the initials "F.C." and the year "1919", and below that the initials "P.H.".

An assortment of initials and dates can be seen in the rock from the West end of the cliffs. In the upper left is the year "1919", and below that is the initials "P.H.", and in the upper right corner are the initials "F.H.". Below that is the year "1920", and to the left of that are another set of initials or date, but the stone has flaked away and it is impossible to make anything out. Below that in the left corner the last three letters of a name, "LER", can be made out. We would guess that it is the remains of "Sheffler", and since it has all been framed in, we are assuming that these etchings are from "P.H.Sheffler" and "F.H.Sheffler" from 1920. The weathering of this rock can be plainly seen in these photographs.

The initials "J.E." and "H.S." above, are the largest etchings we found along the cliffs. They measure about five inches high and are carved deep in to the rock.

These initials are above and to the left of all the initials on the previous pages.

The year or date above was found just to the right of the J.E. and H.S. initials. At a quick glance it appears to be the year "1712". But after studying it awhile, the first and last number look to be the same.

It could be the year "71" with some scrolling on either side, or another guess would be "2-7-12", for February 7, 1912.

We are kind of leaning towards the last one, 2-7-12, but there is no proof to back that up, just a guess by us.

THE FENNELL FAMILY

In the photo above you can plainly make out "Bill Fennell, 1931". We found this on a low rock as we moved East along the trail.

John Fennell and his wife Elizabeth owned a piece of property approximately three to four miles West of New Alexandria, where the town of Fennelltown was established.

In the early 1800's, the Fennell family built a church in which the Lutherans and the Reformed Church held their services on alternating Sabbaths. Eventually, the Reformed Church members erected their own building.

Michael Fennell, son of John and Elizabeth, married

Susan Fennell, a second cousin, and they had a son named Jacob.

Jacob Fennell was married to Anise H. McWherter, and they had the following children; Dora, Abbie, Sarah, Hazel, Ira, Homer, and Charlie. We could find no reference to a Bill or William Fennell other than a W. Fennell listed in the 1867 Atlas of Westmoreland County as owning property near Fennelltown in Loyalhanna Township.

We are not sure how William is related to the rest of the family, only that it is obvious that he lived during the 1931 time period, when he carved his name in the cliffs.

Other Fennells that we have found are Carl Fennell, Warren Fennell, and Ruth Fennell, who were all registered as attending the New Alexandria school in 1912.

There also was a P.S. Fennell listed as owning and operating a Livery stable in New Alexandria, and also advertising automobiles for hire. He worked as a Justice of the Peace, and his barn was located just behind the Post Office.

There was also an L.H. Fennell listed as being a building contractor in the early days of New Alexandria. They must have been a predominate family in the area as the main road through Salemville is named Fennell Street.

The initials "J.P.G. 1929", these were the last ones we found on the West end.

THE BEGINNING OF NEW ALEXANDRIA

In 1757, a Mrs. Moore and her son John settled at the mouth of Crabtree Run, and became the first settler's of what was to become Derry Township. In 1760, William Bulbridge tomahawked a claim on the ground that would become New Alexandria. For a long period of time he lived in peace with the Indians, for they still considered this their ground.

The initials "G.B." found on Signature Rock along the Loyalhanna

Later on, in 1763, to put a temporary halt to Indian hostilities, the British enacted "The Proclamation Line of 1763", which effectively drew a line at a 45 degree angle up through Pennsylvania with Fort Ligonier being on the Western edge of this. It forbade any settlements West of that line. But some settlers like the Moore's and Bulbridge ignored this and settled there anyway. William Bulbridge was eventually killed by an Indian for his rifle.

The name "Chas. Bell", (Charles Bell), on Signature Rock.

Thomas Bulbridge, William's brother, came from Cumberland County and settled on his late brothers claim. When the Land Office opened in 1769, he took out a warrant for this claim. He later sold it in 300 acre parcels, one to Lt. Samuel Craig, and the other to Arthur Denniston.

Samuel Craigs property was on the West side of the Loyalhanna Creek, and Arthur Denniston's property reached from the East side of Loyalhanna to the Post office. Alexander Denniston owned the property from the Post Office to where the present borough line is today.

The initials "T.M." carved in to Signature Rock

Arthur began laying out a settlement and called it Dennistontown, and Alexander began doing the same in 1793 calling his the New Town of Alexandria.

In 1834 the two were incorporated and named New Alexandria. After the Land Office opened in April 1769, the settlers began pouring in, filing their claims, each eager to own their own piece of ground.

Above, is the letter "H", the second letter appears to be "N" or "H". The initials "H.W." below, both from Signature Rock.

The initials "B.S." above and "E.R.S." below, both found on Signature Rock.

Above, "P.H.", and below "M.S. '79" below, both are on Signature Rock.

The initials "T.W.S." below and "R.S.- May, 18??" above.

The initials "I.M." above, and "J.B." below on Signature Rock.

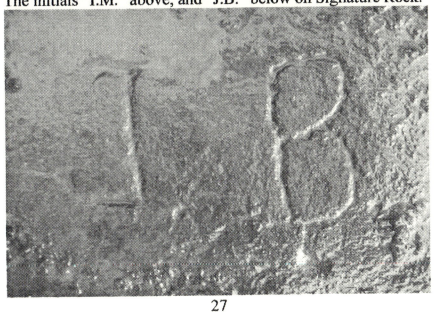

Also from Signature Rock, "L.T." above and "J.S.S." below.

Above are the initials "G.W.S.", also from Signature Rock. The letters are just barely visible. When the Loyalhanna Creek is high, the rock is completely underwater and as you can see from this photograph, the current from the water is slowly eroding it away.

These are all of the etchings that we found on Signature Rock. As we have stated previously, it must have been a favorite meeting place for everyone. It is the only group of large boulders found along the creek behind New Alexandria.

All of the initials were carved in to the top of the rock, with the exception of "Chas. Bell", which is on the side, and affords it some protection from the current.

The initials "G.W." above, and "C.M." below are on the cliff.

Above, "G.G.L." and below "G.S.", both from the Cliffside.

The initials "L.L." below are carved deep into the rock, while above you can just see the letter "P". The rest is worn away.

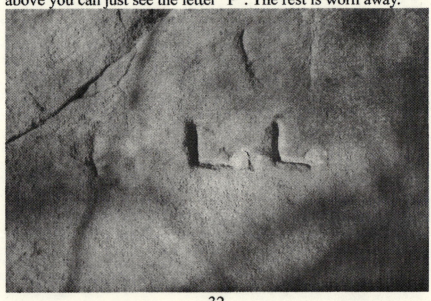

The large accumulation of initials above are high up on the cliff, and were missed on our first few trips along the trail. When we decided to go down and record everything we could find, we started looking in places that we hadn't before.

They are about seven to eight feet above our heads. The rock that formed the overhang that these persons stood on to carve them has broken away. We used a zoom lens to take this photograph.

At the top is "A.B.S.", under that is "L.? O.", couldn't make out the middle letter. Under that is "J.H.S.", and then "H. ? E.", another that we couldn't make out the middle letter. Under that is "F.I.", and at the top right is "P.H. '84". (1884). The white blotches are a form of Lichen growing on the rock.

In this photograph can be seen "FFLER, FEB 23, 1882". The "LER" can be plainly seen, while the "FF" is barely visible. The year "1882" can also be made out clearly, while the month and day took some close up deciphering. The first part of the Sheffler name is gone, along with any first name initials. This was on the cliff about three quuarters of the way along the trail.

THE SHEFFLER FAMILY

The Sheffler family has roots in New Alexandria going back to almost 1800. John Abner Sheffler, (1802-1853), and his wife Elizabeth, (1800-1874), lived in Elderton, Pennsylvania where they operated a blacksmith shop. John is buried in

The name "M.T. Sheffler" above along the top, and below that to the left is "LER", the remains of another Sheffler name. These are on the cliff about half way along the trail.

Elderton, while his wife is buried in the cemetery by the Presbyterian Church on Church Street in New Alexandria.

Their son Jacob A. Sheffler, (1827-1900), came to New Alexandria in 1860 where he was married to Barbara Ann Prugh in that same year. She died in 1913.

Jacob followed in his father's footsteps and opened a blacksmith shop in a building next to his home on Main Street in New Alexandria.

Above is "J.E. SHEFFLER, MAY 9, 1886" from the cliffs.

Later this would become an auto garage as the automobile began replacing the horse and buggy.

Jacob and Barbara had ten children: Cyrus F., James H., William A., Sampson H., Charles M., Lizzie P., John Abner, Oliver Grant, Annabell, and Edward.

Oliver's family and descendants are: Stewart Sheffler, Harold Sheffler, Dean Sheffler, Robert Sheffler, Wayne Sheffler, Mary Sheffler, James Laughlin, Alex O.Laughlin, Goldie Chicka, and Betty Chicka.

Edward Sheffler's descendants are: Stanley J., Edward W., Stanley E., Pearl Pinchok, Eva Moyer, Doris Hugus,

John Berger, Lillian Berger, and Julia Yingst.

Robert Sheffler was married to Christina Grimm, and their children are: Christina, Ruth, Patricia, and Robert Jr.

Robert Jr.'s children are: Julie Ann, Robert Grant, and Michelle.

Walter and Nettie Sheffler's children are: Walter Jr., James Paul, Lloyd, and Charles Wayne.

More Sheffler etchings above, on top is "J.H. Sheffler, April 1, 1871". Below that is "S.H. Sheffler, April 11, 1871". Below that to the right is "A. Sligh". These are on the cliff about half way along the trail.

Sheffler family reunion, August 12, 1906

All of the Sheffler's children, also had children over the years, so you can imagine the size of the Sheffler family, their relatives, and descendants in the New Alexandria area and the impact they had on this community. The photograph on the previous page gives you an idea just how large this family was.

The photograph was taken on August 12, 1906, and is printed here by courtesy of our neighbor, Julia (Jill) Yingst, one of Edward J. Sheffler's descendants.

These initials on the cliffs are starting to fade away. You can still make out the letters "I.S.".

This is a closer view of the "A. SLIGH" etching.

ALEXANDER HALIDAY SLIGH

Alexander Haliday Sligh was born near Berwick on Tweed in Scotland, and came to America at the age of twenty-one. He married Lucinda Hannah McConnell, whose family lived on a farm near the Old Congruity Church. He built a house in New Alexandria, where their first daughter, Janet Guthrie Sligh, was born. Seven years later the house was sold and he bought a house on Church St., diagonally across from the schoolhouse, (now a playground), where their second daughter, Martha Agnes Sligh, was born.

This house was sold, and Alexander bought a house on the corner of Church Street and Washington Street, across from the present day Newhouse Funeral Home. He learned the trade of Stone Mason in Scotland, and for several years he owned a General Store in New Alexandria. He was an Elder in the Presbyterian Church which was just across the street from his home.

Both of his daughters attended Indiana Normal School, now Indiana University of Pennsylvania, and both of them became teachers in New Alexandria. Martha married James Lyall Turnbull in 1918, and they moved to Maplewood, New Jersey. Under the name Agnes Sligh Turnbull, she wrote many short stories for various magazines, and twenty-seven books, some pertaining to her life in New Alexandria. Her sister Janet remained a teacher and wrote two books of her own.

The initials "R.S. 1961" also about half way along the cliffs.

Above, "D.H.R.-I.B.G. and A.B.C." found on the cliff.

"REX BELBOURNE, '39 DEC".

The initials "J.P." above and "W" below. Nothing else seems to be associated with the one below.

Two etchings that are showing wear. Above is "N.L." on top and an "M.?" below that. Can't make the second letter out. Photo below is completely unrecognizable because of weathering.

More etchings that have faded with time. Two more reasons why we decided to do a photographic record of them.

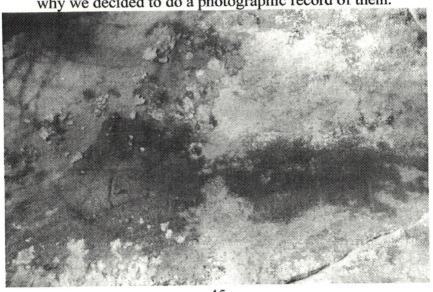

A turn of the century photo of New Alexandria on the West side of the Loyalhanna Creek.

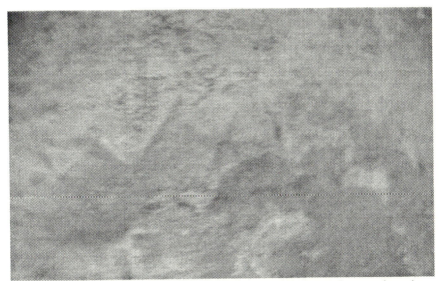

The initials "C.H." below and "W.A." above. Both are showing some wear from time and weather.

The name "MUNSON" etched in to the side of the cliff.

MUNSON

James Munson was born on June 14, 1891 and was the son of James M. and Mary Kull Munson of New Alexandria. James was an active member in the Presbyterian Church and eventually became a teacher in the Salem Township School District.

James was married in 1919 to Eleanor R. Felton of West Middlesex. They moved to Uniontown, PA: then to Point Marion, PA, and finally settled in New Castle, PA. They did not have any children.

The initials "L.P." on the cliffs are starting to fade away.

AD IN THE FAYATTE COUNTY GAZETTE
OCT. 29, 1793

"The New Town Alexandria, Penna.--is lately laid out on the Eastern bank of the Loyalhanning Creek about eight miles from the place where it joins the river Conemaugh, and forms the Kiskiminetas near the center of Westmoreland County, and on the state road leading from Frankstown to Pittsburgh about twenty-six miles from the latter. It is a beautiful level situation and in one of the best settlements of land in the Western country.

The initials "G.E.G." can still be seen in the photo above.

There is an excellent merchant mill and saw mill adjoining the town and the transportation easy for Kentucky boats of any size down the Loyalhanning Creek into Kiskimenetas; In the center of said town is a handsome public square, one hundred and eighty feet each way, the streets are sixty feet wide, one extending from the creek along the state road, two parallel with it, one on each side and one crossing them at right angles, thru the public square.

There are ninety-three lots laid out, each sixty feet in front and one hundred and sixty-one feet in depth, except the diamond lots, which are sixty feet in front and one hundred and one feet deep. On the side of each lot there is an alley of six feet wide and one of eight feet at the end of each. The price of lots will be three pounds and ten shillings each one-half to be paid on making the application, and the other when the deed in fee simple shall be executed. Tickets will be prepared and a lottery for preference drawn on Friday the fifteenth of next month on the premises. Such persons as may become purchasers and cannot conveniently attend in persons, will please to nominate others to draw for them. Alex Denniston".

"H 39" can be seen above, but is also showing signs of wear from weathering.

"J.D.B. above and "R.L." below are starting to erode away but can still be made out plainly.

The name "J. FELTON", belonging to either James or John Felton, the sons of William and Adeline Felton.

THE FELTON FAMILY

William Felton was born in 1803, and was married to a McAllister. He died in 1828. William made his living as a stage coach driver, contractor, carpenter, cabinet maker, and finally got in to the trade of making coffins.

They had a son, William M. Felton Jr., born on January 4, 1827 and died on July 20, 1901. He married Adeline Johnston, who was born in 1835, and died in 1920. William and Adeline had eight children; James L. born in 1854,

William H. born in 1856, John S. born in 1858, Mary E. born in 1862, Ada B. born in 1864, McAllister W. born in 1867, Charles E. born in 1869, and Edward R. born in 1873.

McAllister married Nancy Mae Fennell and they had two children; Mary Felton Pierce Hart born in 1896, and died in 1941, and McAllister Wallace Felton Jr. born on October 13, 1898, and died on May 22, 1974. McAllister Jr. was married to Mary M. McFayden who was born on November 8, 1911, and they had three children; Nancy Louise Binidy born in 1932, McAllister W. III born in 1937, and Dr Craig McFayden Felton born in 1938.

Below is the name "Willard Huld, DEC ??", the year could not be made out. We could not find any information for this name.

McAllister Wallace Felton Jr. graduated from the Washington and Jefferson College and Eckles School of Embalming.

Edward R. Felton began and operated a funeral home business in New Alexandria up until 1895, when McAllister W. Felton Sr. bought it. Edward was one of the first licensed undertakers in Westmoreland County.

McAllister W. Felton Jr. joined with his father in the business in 1922.

Below are the initials "J.P." with what looks to be "NOV", the abbreviation for November but with a backwards "N". Below that is hard to make out, probably remains of a date and year.

Up until 1925 it was operated out of the Gray Wing Hall building at the West end of town, and the coffins were built in the structure in the rear before moving to the Kaufman house on Main Street. McAllister Jr. owned and operated a funeral home in Blairsville, PA from 1928 to 1932, and then returned to New Alexandria, PA in 1935. The funeral home was then operated from the McCartney home on the West side of the Loyalhanna Creek, and they ran the business there until 1941 when it was moved to the Patterson home on the corner of Washington Street and Church Street.

Below, the initials "K.C. 89" can be seen. The etching above it, which is fairly long, is worn off enough that we could not make out what it was.

McAllister W. Felton Jr. died in 1974, and Clayton Linsley took over as temporary supervisor in February of 1975, and then supervisor in May of 1975. The funeral home is still operating today on the East corner of Washington and Church Streets, and is presently owned by David Newhouse.

Below are the initials "K.I."

The initials "C.G." above. "N.O." can be seen below. We are not sure if the third letter is "L" or possibly a "V".

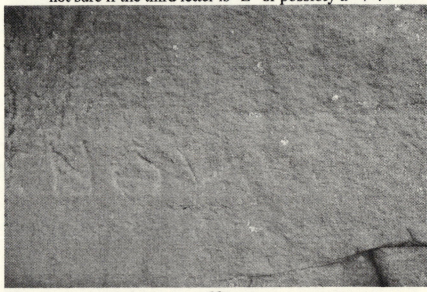

The name "P. King, APR 20, ????" above. Could be that of Patrick King, we could not make out any part of the year.

THE KING FAMILY

Frank King was born and raised in the East end area of Pittsburgh, PA. He married Adaline McConnell of Cresson, PA whose family owned and operated a dairy farm. After their marriage, they moved in to a home in Wilkinsburg, PA. In 1949, the Kings purchased a farm from Curtis Shirey on the Hannastown Road, and moved there in 1950.

In 1962 the King's purchased the property of Walter Porter in New Alexandria. Their son Patrick (Pat) King, married Kathy Callahan from Latrobe, and they resided on the farm on Hannastown Road with their two sons, Patrick Jr. and Timothy.

Frank's daughter Delee L. King, was a school teacher in the Greensburg Salem School District, and she lived in Greensburg, PA.

Below, the name "PAT", could be that of Patrick King Jr. who was known by the nickname Pat.

We have found a J. King, listed in the 1867 Atlas of Westmoreland County, as owning property on the Northwest corner of the intersection of Main Street, School Street, and Saltsburg Street, diagonally across from the present day Post Office.

Below is "J. KING, DEC. 18. '39". This is on one of the rocks that originally formed an overhang but has broken away and is on the ground at the base of the cliff.